NEVER Cut Costs.......

Tim Levey

ISBN:
ISBN-978-1-4467-2631-0

DEDICATION

to Philip Gabriel Levey,

the Best Dad a Son could have

INTRODUCTION TO THE CAST (in order of appearance)

Cher Holder – a second generation lifestyle business owner of Holder Holdings.

Cher only owns the business because her dear departed father set it up and ran it successfully for many years until his sudden death. As an only child her father had spoilt her throughout his life. With this in mind he had developed a neat systematic way of working so that the business could actually run without him, although he rarely tested this. Cher uses this to her advantage and leaves the staff who worked the system under her father to carry on as they did previously. She remains unmarried and lives happily on her own with a cat. Her £1,000 per week salary means that meals could generally be eaten out, usually at the golf course where she is a previous Ladies' Captain.

Loyal – Administration Assistant

Ever since she started working for Mr. Holder after she left school, she has been one of the first people in every morning and one of the last to leave. All of her work follows the system that Mr. Holder encouraged her to develop for herself. She quietly gets on with her work. This means that by the end of Friday afternoon she has already prepared the accounts for the week, ready for the results to be reviewed first thing on the Monday morning.

Antonio Hemming – Consultant

He worked in a bank for many years, but reached the age where he was far too experienced to stay! Having been "retired" on a full pension, aged just 50, he answered a newspaper advert that was looking for franchisees for a national Business Consulting Network. After paying a large amount of money to go on a residential training course, he read a number of books and manuals that had been written by the individual who had set up the network and at the end of the week he got a certificate saying that he was a "Qualified Consultant".

Philip Gabriel – a P.R.O.F.I.T. Coach

He spent many years running businesses for other people and at his last employment realised that he had been working a system that earned his bosses a fortune, while he was left on a salary and a small bonus. Having finally paid off his mortgage, he retired and lived on his savings while he captured the system in writing. He now offers help to small business owners who have lost their way.

Supervisor – Operations Manager

Like *Loyal*, he joined Mr. Holder from school many years ago and has not worked anywhere else. He helped to develop the system and enjoys the nice steady life that has resulted from this. His most usual comment is "it doesn't matter to me", when actually it does.

Greedy – Machine Operative

He has not been at Holder Holdings very long. In fact, he does not stay in any job very long and he is always annoying management with his constant demands for more money. Not only will you need a carrot to encourage this donkey to move, he will want to eat it first as well!

Disruptive – Deliveryman

Some people just can't help themselves. He can see the worst case in every situation and then will share his thoughts and fears with everyone that he comes into contact with. He speaks without any thought for the consequences and is at his happiest when everyone is annoyed with him.

Sociable – Salesman

With a smile in his voice and on his face, everyone feels good when he's around. Customers look forward to his visits and his charming manner means that they rarely refuse his sales proposals.

Price – an existing customer

There is no point in talking about quality and service to this customer. There is only one thing that he wants and that is the cheapest possible price. He does, however, pay very quickly, especially if there's an early settlement discount on offer.

Demanding – a new customer

They will be high maintenance. Calls need to be answered quickly and top quality products will need to be delivered exactly when they were promised. On the other side, they are willing to pay for top quality goods and services.

Impatient – a new customer

You'll have to be ready to gets your skates on with them. They leave everything to the last minute, so when they make an order, you'll have to get working on it straight away.

Lo-Quality – a new supplier

If good quality is required, then you would be better off going elsewhere. They source their materials from the rejects that others will not touch, and then pass them off as the same but cheaper.

No Hassle – the existing supplier

They bend over backwards to help their customers and keep their promises. A good supplier to have if you are in a spot of bother or just want an easy life. Not the cheapest on the market, but then who wants that?

Quality – an existing customer

They are willing to pay for top quality material and will not tolerate the slightest defects or inaccuracies in deliveries.

Delivery – an existing customer

They want it accurate, they want it on time and they are happy to pay for it. Little else matters.

Angel – an existing customer

Your perfect customer. They are polite to a fault, pay all of their bills on time and never complain. They are so easy it's quite possible to take them for granted.

Prompt – potential new supplier

They guarantee their scheduled delivery time, which is what they have found is the most important thing to their customers.

Hurry – an existing customer

Another one who wants their order in double quick time. They'll be on the phone before it's due to make sure that it's coming on time. Woe betide you if it's an hour late.

Guaranteed Couriers – same day/ next day delivery

The best way of getting your goods to your more impatient and hurried customers. So good that they never have to pay out on their guaranteed delivery time.

Diligent – Deliveryman

Does the job that needs to be done and does it well, with no complaints. Can be relied upon to get the deliveries done when they are needed.

WorkHorse – Machine Operative

For the hours that he works, you'll get 100% effort and focus on the task in hand. Hard to distract, he does expect his hard work to be recognized in the pay.

Conscientious – Machine Operative

Another one who takes his work very seriously. He'll be in to work early and will not leave until the job is finished to his high standards.

Reliable – Deliveryman

Steady as they come. If you want a good job done, then he'll do it.

ACKNOWLEDGEMENTS

With special thanks to Theresa and Rebecca

Angela West for the cover design; Maria White and Jenny Hinton for editing

Barry Schimel, James Cross and Mark Lloydbottom for the Inspiration

and my Partners at Reeves for their support

WEEK ONE

Cher Holder knew that she was fortunate. She was the owner of a successful business but it took up little of her time. Her father, who had died some 7 years previously, had left her his business, called Holder Holdings. Mr. Holder had been heavily influenced by the management gurus of the day who espoused that business owners who "systematized" their business tended to be more successful than those who did not. He had spent a great deal of time encouraging his staff to plan their work so that predictable results could be obtained with the minimum of effort and these systems were running for a number of years before his sudden death.

Cher had not really worked in the business prior to his death, although as a child she had come in with him during the school holidays and helped to write delivery addresses on labels. While other small business owners worked their fingers to the bone for 6 or even 7 days a week, she followed the system that her father had set up, which meant that she needed to work less than one day each week. Unless she was on holiday, she would visit the business each Monday.

On this particular Monday, she drove her powder blue Mercedes convertible through the gates and parked in her usual place next to the door of the factory. Humming a happy tune, her weeks would start with a quick tour of the premises, talking to all of her staff. She would then look at the accounts for the previous week that were always accurately prepared by *Loyal*, her administration assistant. *Loyal* looked after most things while Cher was away. Cher would then sign the automated payment list that *Loyal* presented, including the payroll for the coming week, and consider any decisions that were needed. Having communicated those decisions to all of the staff, she would then be on her way before lunchtime, fresh for the week ahead which would be taken up with games of golf, networking breakfasts and lunches, and generally taking life easy.

But life needs to have its challenges. And so, on this particular Monday morning, Cher Holder was feeling a sense of déjà vu. For many weeks the accounts that she had looked at on the Monday morning had been absolutely identical to the ones for the previous week.

They were as follows:

	This week	Last week
	£	£
Sales (1,000 units at £10 each)	10,000	10,000
Materials (1,000 units at £4 each)	(4,000)	(4,000)
Direct staff costs (3 at £500 per week)	(1,500)	(1,500)
Gross margin	**4,500**	**4,500**
Indirect staff costs (2 at £500 per week)	(1,000)	(1,000)
Overheads	(1,500)	(1,500)
Cher Holder salary	(1,000)	(1,000)
NET PROFIT	**1,000**	**1,000**

For a long time Cher had been very happy with the 10% net margin that had been achieved. It meant that at the end of each year there was plenty of cash available to pay her tax bill and she could take a dividend of most of the rest, as the business needed little in the way of working capital. Her five customers paid all of their invoices within 14 days and, because materials could be sourced when an order had been received, there was little need to hold any stock. As a result, the business would pay most of its suppliers at the beginning of the week within 30 days of the delivery of the materials.

Recently Cher has become, well, bored, with the monotony of it all. So when in last week's post she came across a neat invitation to a Business Development seminar entitled 'Three Ways to Improve

Profitability', she did something that she had never done before and registered for it.

The seminar was scheduled for that coming Friday morning. After checking her diary, Cher thought that she could squeeze in the time, so she got *Loyal* to make the call and was booked onto it.

Friday's seminar was a revelation. The presenter, Antonio Hemming, presented his material with a great deal of enthusiasm. "There are," he proposed, "just three ways to grow and improve your business and these are the golden questions of business. They come out of the basic equation of business, which says that:

$$\text{Sales volume x price} - \text{costs} = \text{profit}$$

Sales volume, price and costs are therefore the three key profit drivers in any business and therefore the three key questions are:

1. How do you increase your sales volume, by getting customers to buy more or by getting more customers?

2. How do you increase the price of the units that you sell?

3. How do you reduce the costs that you incur?"

He then went through a number of prepared examples showing that just by increasing the number of customers, the order frequency and the order value by 10% each, sales volume would almost magically rise by 61%. And this was all without cutting any costs.

At the break, in the queue for coffee, Cher was standing next to a well-dressed man in his sixties. Cher had noticed him in the audience in the first half, mainly because he was the only person in the room wearing a three piece suit and on his waistcoat was an unusual chain which suggested that he had a pocket watch in his waistcoat. "Wow" said Cher. "That was amazing!"

"Do you think so?" the gentleman replied. "I've heard this stuff so many times before I'm fed up with it. It might sound easy, but be careful how you try and apply this to your own business. I've seen a number of businesses do this badly and cause more damage than good. I'll tell you what. Here's my card. If you try Antonio's ideas and get into trouble then give me a call. The first meeting's always free."

A touch subdued by this comment, Cher read the card that said "Philip Gabriel, helping clients to achieve Perfect P.R.O.F.I.T." Cher thanked Philip for his time, put the card into her pocket and made her way back to her chair for the second half.

Antonio then showed how managing the costs of the business represented the third way to improve profits. "Do all of these together," he exclaimed, "and you have truly achieved the perfect business."

"Fantastic," thought Cher. "I don't care what the other guy thought. I've got nothing to lose by putting some of this into practice next week."

For the first time in goodness knows how long, Cher started to think about the future of the business and the issues that it faced.

WEEK TWO

And so it was that on the next Monday, Cher visited her business, toured the premises and talked to all of her staff. When she got to her office she found the neat page of accounts on her desk as usual. It came as no surprise to her to see the same result as in as many previous weeks as she could remember. Sales of £10,000, resulting in a profit of £1,000.

"Now let's see" thought Cher. "Number 1 was increasing sales volume, but Antonio suggested that this would be the hard one so I'll leave that till later. Number 2 is to get customers to pay more for each unit, which generally means raising the price so that they have to spend more each time they do business with us. Well, that's clearly the easy one. Antonio advised that we should all put our prices up and guaranteed that none of us would regret it, so that's what we shall do."

Cher looked at the matrix that Antonio had provided.

Your gross margin	20%	45%	60%
Proposed increase in price	Sales can decline by	Sales can decline by	Sales can decline by
5%	-20%	-10%	-8%
10%	-33%	-18%	-14%
20%	-50%	-34%	-25%

The business had quite a high gross margin, as the direct staff were really fixed costs, which made it 60%.

"I haven't looked at the prices for some time," thought Cher. "I think that a 20% rise should do the trick. I would have to lose two customers to be worse off, but I think that's unlikely. Most of them have been with us a long time." Unusually, she decided to call a staff meeting to discuss the plan.

At the staff meeting that followed, the announcement of the immediate price increase met with a mixed reaction.

"It doesn't matter to me," said *Supervisor*.

"Will you pay us more if it works?" said *Greedy*, who worked in the workshop and added the value to the materials.

"I don't think the customers are going to be happy when I tell them" said *Disruptive* the deliveryman.

"You don't have to tell them, I do," exclaimed *Sociable* the salesman. "And I'm not looking forward to it!"

"I think it's a good idea," said *Loyal*, who always seemed to agree with whatever Cher suggested.

"Good, that's settled then", said Cher. "The price per unit goes up to £12 as of now." She signaled that the decision had been made and that everyone could get on with their work.

Cher spent some time signing the cheques that *Loyal* put in front of her. She rarely checked the supporting invoices that were pinned behind, knowing that *Loyal* was rarely wrong.

On her way out, Cher felt wonderful. It was great to have made a real strategic decision for the first time in a long time. One that would put the business on the road to increased profitability and maybe even more leisure time.

She was looking forward to next Monday already.

"Should I let you know how things are going on during the week?" asked *Loyal*, as Cher was preparing to leave.

"I don't think so," said Cher. "I'll catch up next week".

WEEK THREE

Cher bounced in on the next Monday. But on her tour of the premises, she was greeted with a number of glum faces. "What's the matter?" she asked.

It was left to *Sociable* to break the news that one of the customers, **Price**, who always ordered 200 units per week, had rejected the price increase immediately and had taken his order to a competitor. This had meant that everyone had finished their work by Thursday evening and they had all sat around on Friday twiddling their thumbs. *Disruptive* had driven everyone round the bend.

"Oh crumbs," thought Cher. "I'd forgotten all about **Price**. He had been on at me to reduce his prices for some time now. This must have pushed him over the edge. Perhaps I had better call him, apologise for the mistake and put the price back to £10 per unit again."

She dared not look at the accounts that were on her desk, fearing that for the first time in living memory, there would be a loss at the bottom of the page.

To her amazement, the accounts were as follows:

	This week	Last week
	£	£
Sales (800 units at £12 each)	9,600	10,000
Materials (800 units at £4 each)	(3,200)	(4,000)
Direct staff costs (3 at £500 per week)	(1,500)	(1,500)
Gross margin	4,900	4,500
Indirect staff costs (2 at £500 per week)	(1,000)	(1,000)
Overheads	(1,500)	(1,500)
Cher Holder salary	(1,000)	(1,000)
NET PROFIT	**1,400**	**1,000**

"My goodness, it worked after all," she thought. "So sales have gone down 20% but my net profit has gone up 40%! That Antonio is a genius."

Cher sat and thought about her next move. She needed another customer to replace the **Price** work that had gone, but even *Sociable* was unlikely to get results that quickly, so the orders would be down this week again.

She went back to the notes that she had taken from the seminar and looked again at the central equation. Having accepted that the volume could not go up quickly, and having increased the price only last week, the only variable to consider was the costs.

"Well, there is one thing that we could do this week. If there is only 800 units expected, then there is some spare capacity that is not going to be used."

Cher then called a staff meeting and informed *Supervisor*, *Greedy* and *Disruptive* that they would have to take Friday off unpaid this week, but that *Sociable* would surely bring a new customer in for the following week.

None of them were particularly happy about losing the money, but reasoned that doing what they wanted to at home would be better than getting bored at work.

With the meeting closed, Cher left; certain in the knowledge that with the savings made on the direct salaries, the profits should continue to increase next week.

WEEK FOUR

Perhaps surprisingly, morale seemed to be much better the following Monday.

Sociable had been able to recruit not one but two new customers, **Demanding** and **Impatient**, during the week and the first orders for 200 units each were coming in this week. The direct staff had therefore enjoyed their long weekend, safe in the knowledge that they would soon be back on full time and full pay. They could even be getting overtime!

This week the accounts on Cher's desk told the story that she would have predicted:

	This week	Last week
	£	£
Sales (800 units at £12 each)	9,600	9,600
Materials (800 units at £4 each)	(3,200)	(3,200)
Direct staff costs (3 at £400 per week)	(1,200)	(1,500)
Gross margin	**5,200**	**4,900**
Indirect staff costs (2 at £500 per week)	(1,000)	(1,000)
Overheads	(1,500)	(1,500)
Cher Holder salary	(1,000)	(1,000)
NET PROFIT	**1,700**	**1,400**

"Brilliant", thought Cher. "We've done 20% less sales than when I started on this journey and the profits have gone up 70%. This gets better all the time!"

She then thought about what the results were going to be for next week. The extra 400 units from **Demanding** and **Impatient** would generate a gross profit of £8 each or £3,200, against which there would be more direct staff costs of £600 at the worst. If she did nothing else the profits next week would be £4,300!

Cher flicked through the notes from the seminar. Having had some real success with increasing the price of each sale and increasing the sales volume, it was time to look at the costs again. The biggest cost was of materials.

"This is going to be easy", thought Cher. "I've had other suppliers leaving messages for me for some time. Where are all those numbers?" In a pile in her drawer she found messages and phone numbers for the salesmen of three suppliers. She also found the card that the stranger that she met in the break at the seminar had given her. "Ha! I won't be needing that," she said throwing it back in the drawer.

A few hours later, Cher had done a deal with a new supplier. **Lo-Quality** were willing to work on the same terms as the existing supplier, but at the rate of just £2 per unit! Cher had tried to get the existing supplier, **No Hassle**, to match this, but they would only go down as low as £3, with a guaranteed contract for 12 months. "**Lo-Quality** doesn't require a 12 month commitment," Cher reasoned. "We have to go with them."

Cher called all the staff into her office for the usual chat. "I've decided to use a different supplier in future," she announced. "They are going to supply the same materials to us, but for half the existing price."

"It doesn't matter to me," said *Supervisor*, shrugging his shoulders.

"Won't the customers realise that there's been a change?" asked *Disruptive*.

"Not if you don't tell them," said *Sociable*.

"Mmm, sounds like a good deal," said *Loyal*.

"Good, let's get on with it," said Cher.

As everyone continued about their business, Cher signed the cheques with a flourish and with that, she left for the week.

WEEK FIVE

Cher could hardly wait for the next Monday morning. She even arrived at the business a bit earlier than usual as she was so keen to see what the results would be like. She went straight to find *Loyal*.

"How is everyone?" she asked *Loyal*.

"Well, they're a bit up and down actually," said *Loyal*. "The first part of the week was OK, but by Wednesday we were getting a lot of calls from customers saying that the parts we supplied are not as good as they have been. One in five of them got sent back and we had to order some more from **Lo-Quality** and work a bit of overtime to get them processed and delivered."

"Oh dear," said Cher, "perhaps I've gone too far this time. Show me what the accounts look like."

Loyal placed the sheet in front of her:

	This week	Last week
	£	£
Sales (1,200 units at £12 each)	14,400	9,600
Materials (1,400 units at £2 each)	(2,800)	(3,200)
Direct staff costs (3 at £700 per week)	(2,100)	(1,200)
Gross margin	**9,500**	**5,200**
Indirect staff costs (2 at £500 per week)	(1,000)	(1,000)
Overheads	(1,500)	(1,500)
Cher Holder salary	(1,000)	(1,000)
NET PROFIT	**6,000**	**1,700**

"But this is brilliant!" exclaimed Cher. "Even with the extra materials and labour costs, we've still managed to increase profitability. I'm making 600% more than I did before I went to the seminar."

"Before you get too carried away," said *Loyal*, "the staff want to see you as soon as you get in."

"Yes, of course," said Cher. "I should have gone to see them first. I'll get straight out there."

The first person that she saw was *Supervisor*. He got straight to the point. "You must change back to **No Hassle**" he said. "The quality of these new parts is terrible. It's been chaos here with the rejections. What with getting more new materials in to replace the bad parts and working overtime to process the new materials, I've been rushed off my feet. My wife has hardly seen me this week."

Cher waved his concerns away. "There's no way we're changing back to the old supplier", she said. "I'm sure these are just teething problems which will get better in the next few weeks. You're getting overtime. You can treat your wife to something to make-up can't you?"

"I suppose so", said *Supervisor*, "but this can't go on for much longer."

Sociable was the next person to see her. "I'm worried about next week's orders," he said. "**Quality** and **Demanding** both mentioned the poor quality and said that unless things improved they would be looking elsewhere for their parts."

"Don't worry about them," said Cher, putting a comforting arm around *Sociable's* shoulder. "As I've just told *Supervisor*, these quality issues are just teething problems. Give it a few weeks and things will be back to normal."

"I do hope you're right," said *Sociable*, who looked far from convinced.

Next up was *Greedy*. "Are you going to comment about the quality issues as well?" asked Cher, "because I think everything's been covered already."

"Not really," said *Greedy*. "The overtime's been quite useful really, but I've been doing some sums and I reckon that you're making a hell of a lot more money than you used to. I think it's about time that you gave us all a pay rise to share it around a bit."

Cher was quite taken aback by this. She thought for a while before remarking "But it was only a few months ago that the annual review took place. You'll have to wait until the next one before I see what we can afford."

"Well, what about a bonus in the meantime" asked *Greedy*.

"Certainly not!" retorted Cher. "You're getting overtime, that should be enough."

"Well, just to warn you" said *Greedy*. "Unless there's news of a pay rise or a bonus next week, I'm off!" And with that he turned on his heel.

"What an ungrateful person" said Cher, shaking her head in disbelief. "Unbelievable."

Disruptive had already started his deliveries by this time, which meant that Cher didn't get to see him.

The episode with *Greedy* in particular had shaken Cher.

Loyal was waiting in her office when she got back. "Any changes this week?" she asked.

"I don't think so" said Cher with a grimace. "I haven't got enough time to put anything into action and until these quality issues quieten down, nobody here is going to have the time to do anything out of the ordinary either."

Then after reflection she said. "There's just one thing though. When you're doing the payroll on Friday, give me an extra £1,000. I think I've deserved it this week."

Cher signed the other cheques while *Loyal* made the necessary changes to the payroll, and with that, she left with a spring in her step.

WEEK SIX

Cher arrived the next Monday to find that *Greedy* was waiting for her in her office. This was a bit unusual. It was only when she saw him that she remembered their conversation the previous week.

As usual, *Greedy* was very direct. "Have you thought about the rise that I asked for last week?"

"Well, no" replied Cher in all honesty.

"So, what are you going to do?" he persisted.

"I'm not proposing to do anything until next year" Cher replied.

"Right, I'm off then" said *Greedy* standing up to go.

"You can't just go", said Cher. "You've got to work your notice period."

"Hard luck" replied *Greedy*. "If you can't be fair with me, then I can't be bothered to be fair with you! I've got another job fixed up already." He turned and went.

Cher was a bit stunned by this and so waited for a bit before she went out to see the other staff. They had known that *Greedy* was going to cause some trouble and had been keeping out of the way.

When Cher went out into the workshop she found *Disruptive* clowning around as usual. "Haven't you got enough work to do" she asked.

"Actually, no" said *Disruptive* cheekily.

"Why on earth not?" asked Cher.

"Well, we had so many problems with the raw material quality last week that some of the customers cancelled their orders midway through the week."

Cher went straight off to find *Sociable*. She found him in his office with the door shut and on the phone. It was clear that *Sociable* was on the phone to a customer – or was it an ex-customer? Cher went in quietly and let *Sociable* carry on with his conversation.

"I can only apologise for the quality of the parts that you've received in the last few weeks" he spluttered. "We're working as hard as we can to rectify these faults and you can be assured that we will continue to replace any that you've found to be defective… Yes, I know that this has caused you problems with your own customers. In fact, Miss Holder has just come through the door and I'm about to discuss the position with her now. Can I give you a call back just as soon as I have finished?"

Sociable put the phone down. "That was **Quality**", he said. "Unfortunately he says that it's too late for us to do anything about getting him back – he is going to another supplier today! I had a similar conversation with **Demanding** late last week. He said it was disgraceful that I had promised so much when I first went to see him and had then under-delivered so badly since."

"What are you going to do about getting some new customers?" asked Cher.

"I don't know. If word has got out into the market about our quality problems then it's going to be very hard," said *Sociable*.

"Well, try your hardest," said Cher. "Things have been really good these last few weeks, but I need more sales to keep the momentum going. I'm relying on you!"

Cher saw *Supervisor* on her way back to her office. "I suppose you know that *Greedy* has gone?" she said.

"Yes," said *Supervisor*. "It's probably just as well. He was only ever after whatever he could get out of the place. It was only while the business was stable that he stopped trying to grab overtime for himself. We'll be better off without him. Do you want me to find a replacement?"

"Not just yet," said Cher. "I'll just go and have a look at last week's figures and work out what this week might look like with two customers gone."

True to form, *Loyal* had left the accounts on her desk:

	This week	Last week
	£	£
Sales (1,000 units at £12 each)	12,000	14,400
Materials (1,300 units at £2 each)	(2,600)	(2,800)
Direct staff costs (3 at £650 per week)	(1,950)	(2,100)
Gross margin	**7,450**	**9,500**
Indirect staff costs (2 at £500 per week)	(1,000)	(1,000)
Overheads	(1,500)	(1,500)
Cher Holder salary	(2,000)	(1,000)
NET PROFIT	**2,950**	**6,000**

"Good Grief, what's going on here" she exclaimed. "We made £6,000 last week and it's more than halved!"

Loyal came in with her notes. "Well, **Quality** and **Demanding** only had 100 good parts each delivered this week. They both returned all of their initial deliveries as sub-standard and returned half of the second deliveries too. You can see that we had to order 30% more of the raw materials. I'm not sure if the quality of the materials was worse than last week or whether the customers were checking it more. Anyway, that meant that *Supervisor, Greedy* and *Disruptive* all worked overtime again last week. Oh, and then there was the extra £1,000 that you asked for."

Cher thought carefully about what she saw. She looked ahead to the next week and realised that the sales could only be 800 units at best. She went back to her seminar notes and realised that there was still one thing to be done.

"Right" she said to *Loyal*. "I want you to make cuts into the overheads so that they come down to £1,000 this week."

"But where?" asked *Loyal*. "All the costs have been the same for a long time now. To cut anything is going to have a detrimental effect somewhere."

"I don't care where you make the cuts," said Cher. "Just do it."

"Do you want me to reduce your salary back to £1,000?" asked *Loyal*.

"No way," said Cher. "I'm having to earn it this week!"

Cher went out to see *Supervisor*. "I've been looking at the figures for next week and they don't look good", she said. "It looks like there's only going to be enough work to keep you and *Disruptive* busy until *Sociable* can find some new customers. So I can't afford to have you replace *Greedy* yet. Do you understand? *Disruptive* is going to have to help out with the factory work."

"If you say so", said *Supervisor*. "So long as you know that if we get more rejects this week we'll have to continue the overtime."

"Good point. That reminds me," said Cher. "There'll be no more overtime paid until we get through this."

Before *Supervisor* had a chance to speak, Cher had turned and left.

The spring in her step was absent.

WEEK SEVEN

Cher did not have a good week at all. She had spent the entire time worrying about what she might find when she went in next Monday. She had slept badly and her golf had deteriorated in a big way. Everyone that she met commented that she looked quite unwell – she felt it as well.

In fact she came in much later than usual, when she knew that *Loyal* would have finished checking the accounts. She went straight to her office and shut the door quietly behind her to look at them.

They told a sorry tale:

	This week	Last week
	£	£
Sales (400 units at £12 each)	4,800	12,000
Materials (800 units at £2 each)	(1,600)	(2,600)
Direct staff costs (2 at £500 per week)	(1,000)	(1,950)
Gross margin	**2,200**	**7,450**
Indirect staff costs (2 at £500 per week)	(1,000)	(1,000)
Overheads	(1,000)	(1,500)
Cher Holder salary	(2,000)	(2,000)
NET LOSS	**(1,800)**	**2,950**

"*LOYAL!* What on earth is the meaning of this?" *Loyal* had her notes all ready.

"Not a very good week last week" she understated. "I managed to get the overheads down as you asked, but that meant stopping *Sociable* from doing his direct mailing and changing the stationery order to a cheaper supplier. I've also made the staff pay for their own tea and coffee, which I have to say didn't go down well. I've reduced the insurance cover and cancelled the Permanent Health Insurance and Death in Service policies. I was about to hold back the renewal of your golf club subscription, but all of those things were just enough."

"Yes, yes. But what about the rest of the accounts? These numbers are terrible," exclaimed Cher.

"Well, **Delivery** and **Impatient** cancelled their orders this week. With *Disruptive* being so tied up with manufacturing the parts now that *Greedy* has gone, we were late with the first deliveries of the week, so they both told us not to bother. And as you can see, this week it took two batches of materials to get one unit delivered, so the errors are still going up. Oh, by the way, *Supervisor* and *Sociable* would like to see you."

"Not as much as I'd like to see them," said Cher.

Supervisor came in first. "I suppose you've heard about the bad week that we've had?" he started.

"Yes I have" said Cher. "And I'm waiting to hear what you intend to do to sort things out."

"I'm not sure I can," said *Supervisor*. "The quality of these materials is just so bad that there nothing anyone can do with this. I've been here well into the evening again every day last week, trying as hard as I can to get things out. But as fast as we produce it, the rejects come back - or that's what it seems like anyway."

Cher looked at *Supervisor* closely. Sure enough, his eyes were very red and his normally rosy cheeks were pale. He did look close to breaking point. Laying into him did not seem like a good idea just at the moment, so Cher said that she would think about what to do next and called out for *Sociable* instead. He was certainly due a roasting.

But *Sociable* made it plain that he was not going to take the blame for the poor sales. He had tried to get all of the ex-customers back, but to no avail. He also warned Cher that he had just had a conversation with **Angel,** who said that he had been unable to pass on the higher prices to his customers and might soon have to close down. "I might have been able to recruit some new customers last week," he said, "but you told *Loyal* to cut the overheads and my direct mailing went with it. I haven't been able to send any brochures!"

Cher had heard enough for one day. She opened her drawer, looking for the business cards of her own contacts that she could call. She spent quite a few hours calling old contacts who had received some samples in the past. Sadly, it was clear that word was out in the marketplace and nobody was interested. Then she came across the card that had been given to her by the gentleman at Antonio Hemmings' seminar. The conversation now came back to her. "If you try Antonio's ideas and get into trouble then give me a call. The first meeting's always free" was what he had said. Cher turned the card over and found a message on the back. It simply said:

To achieve Perfect P.R.O.F.I.T.:

"NEVER cut costs .... if the result would be a reduction in customer satisfaction"

"Can you give me a minute *Sociable*?" asked Cher. "I have a call that I need to make." With nothing to lose, Cher called the number on the face of the card.

"Philip Gabriel" said the voice at the other end. "How can I help you?"

"Er, I don't know if you remember me," said Cher. "I met you at the Antonio Hemming seminar a few weeks ago. You gave me your card and told me to call if things didn't work out."

"And I guess they haven't worked out?" asked Philip.

"Well, they did for a while," said Cher defensively, "but things have started to get a bit ragged lately and I could do with some advice. You mentioned that the first meeting was free?"

"Of course," said Philip. "I can't expect you to hire me until I've demonstrated some value. How are you fixed next Monday morning?"

"Well, that's clear at the moment," said Cher, but is there a chance that you can see me earlier? It really is quite urgent."

"Sorry, I'm booked solid until next Monday. I have a number of clients that I see on set days every week and Monday is the only day free at the moment."

"OK then" said Cher. "I don't suppose that things can get much worse before then."

"Excellent, I'll see you next Monday," said Philip before ringing off.

Cher thought about what she was to do before next week. The options were now quite limited.

"*LOYAL!*" she called out.

"Yes, Miss Holder?" said *Loyal* as she came in.

"*Loyal*, I'm going to try changing nothing this week. I've got someone called Philip Gabriel coming in next Monday to see what's what. I'm not sure that he can really help me, but if he arrives before I get here, can you make him welcome?"

"Certainly" said *Loyal*.

It was nearly midday and Cher had had quite enough. She had missed her tee-off time but still decided that the business was going to run better without her being around.

WEEK EIGHT

Cher was surprised that even though she was able to get into the business early on the next Monday, on arrival she was told that her visitor had been there 'for some time'. *Loyal* told her that Philip Gabriel had been waiting at the gates when *Supervisor* arrived at just after 7am and had spent the intervening time looking around the premises and talking to the staff as they arrived.

"He asked me some pretty searching questions" *Loyal* told Cher. "He asked me what had brought me closest to leaving the company and what I would do if I was in charge!"

"Yikes! What did you say to that?" asked Cher.

"I didn't know quite what to say, so I played safe and said very little," said *Loyal*, true to form.

"I think that I'd better go and find him," said Cher.

"Before you do, here are last week's accounts," said *Loyal*.

	This week	Last week
	£	£
Sales (200 units at £12 each)	2,400	4,800
Materials (300 units at £2 each)	(600)	(1,600)
Direct staff costs (2 at £500 per week)	(1,000)	(1,000)
Gross margin	**800**	**2,200**
Indirect staff costs (2 at £500 per week)	(1,000)	(1,000)
Overheads	(1,000)	(1,000)
Cher Holder salary	(2,000)	(2,000)
NET LOSS	**(3,200)**	**(1,800)**

Cher looked at the accounts, but her comments were unprintable. "What on earth has been happening" she shrieked. "I leave you all here to look after the business and look what happens."

"Well, at least the rejects rate came down," said *Loyal*. "Having said that, the only sales were to **Angel**, who tends to be rather more forgiving than the other customers that we've had. He only sent back half of his delivery as sub-standard. *Sociable* called a lot of potential new customers but he said that without the first mailshot it's really difficult. He got fed up on Friday and went home early."

"I thought I'd told you to forget about the overhead cuts?" said Cher.

"Er, no. You told me to keep everything as it was," replied *Loyal*.

"Did I? I suppose I must have done," said Cher, knowing that *Loyal* was always right in these matters. "OK, I'd better go and find this guy."

"One final thing before you go," said *Loyal* sheepishly. "*Sociable* phoned in this morning. He said that he's had enough and won't be coming back."

Cher gave a sound that, if it could be best described, would have been exasperation.

Philip Gabriel was listening earnestly to *Disruptive* when Cher found him. "It looks like I've found you just in time," said Cher, extending a hand in welcome. "You can't believe everything *Disruptive* tells you."

"Oh, I don't know," said Philip, who gave a firm handshake. "Everyone has told me a lot of interesting things while I have been here."

"Come back to my office," said Cher. "We can talk in more privacy there."

When they had settled down in the comfortable leather chairs in Cher's room, it was Philip who got the ball rolling. "So, tell me what has been happening since we met at the seminar?"

In as much detail as she could remember, Cher related the events of the past few weeks. She punctuated this by showing Philip the weekly accounts that had been the result of each week's decisions, before sitting back and waiting for his considered opinion.

"Before we go any further", said Philip. "I want to set out my terms of engagement. They are quite simple but I'm afraid that they aren't negotiable. They are:

- You will agree each Monday whether or not you want me to continue for a further 7 days. Our contract therefore runs for a week at a time;

- If you ignore any of my advice during a week then you must accept that I can and will terminate the contract with immediate effect;

- You will start to put in a proper week's work. This is your business after all; and

- On the final Monday, you will pay me 7% of any additional profits that have been generated from now, multiplied by the number of weeks that I am involved."

"That seems fair," said Cher. "It looks like I do need help. How do we get going?"

"I've taken the liberty of bringing an engagement letter along," said Philip, taking one piece of paper out of his folder. "Have a look through it and sign at the bottom." Cher did so with her usual flourish.

"How much time do we have?" asked Philip, looking at the watch that he pulled out of his waistcoat pocket.

"Oh, as much time as you need" answered Cher, conscious that he had just asked her to start getting more serious about the hours that she was putting in.

"OK, now to get started, what are you going to do without *Sociable?*" Philip asked.

"I haven't had time to think about it," said Cher. "I suppose I'd better recruit another salesman."

"Not much point, when you don't have a great product to sell" suggested Philip. "Well, for number one, it seems clear that you've broken my first rule of profit improvement, which is 'Never cut costs if the result could be a reduction in customer satisfaction'."

"Right, I remember," said Cher, taking the card out the drawer again and reading it.

"It's all very well for Antonio Hemming to focus people on cutting costs, but too many people do this at random and without thinking through the implications of their actions."

"What exactly does Perfect P.R.O.F.I.T. mean?" asked Cher, still looking at the card. "Is it the point where profits are maximised?"

"Not quite," replied Philip. "But it's a good question and deserves a good answer. Have you studied economics at all?"

"Yes, I struggled through a course in it at college," said Cher.

"Good, then you should have come across the idea of 'perfect competition'. This is where there are many buyers and sellers, a homogenous product, sufficient knowledge in the market and no barriers to entry. Intense competition therefore drives down the price of goods so that the benefit is with the consumer rather than the producer. Very few examples of this exist although this textbook model may actually be getting more achievable as time goes on. The Internet and the global market has broken the barriers of distance and imperfect information, so that it's not so easy to charge a premium price.

Now the net profit that goes to shareholders such as you may be an element of Perfect P.R.O.F.I.T., and an important one. However, I would suggest that the focus on the bottom line alone would, as you have experienced, be a strictly short term one. There must be more to the picture if the Profitability is to be long term.

If the owners are the first element, the second element concerns the customers, for if the pursuit of the bottom line is at the expense of the customers, then clearly this can only result in just short term gain. You might say that profit is maximised when the ratio of customer satisfaction to customer expectation is 1.001 and so there is a small amount of over-delivery each time.

Thirdly, you can always start a healthy chicken and egg debate by asking which is the greatest asset of any business. Most people are smart enough to realise that the things that appear on the balance sheet, property, equipment, stock, debtors and even cash, are rarely, if ever, the greatest asset of the business. There are two competing answers that come to the surface. One has been referred to - the customers. The second is the staff. You then get involved in the circular argument – if you had no customers you lose the staff, but if you have no staff then you soon lose all the customers. The logic of many successful business leaders is to focus first on ensuring that staff are kept happy. If the staff are looked after, they in turn will look after the customers.

There can be little argument that the people come a close second at worst. So certainly the people are the third element of Perfect Profitability. There is also a need to over-deliver to them over the longer term.

So maybe there are actually three "bottom lines". One of these, the return to the owners, is easily visible, whilst the other two are unseen. It then becomes clear that Imperfect Profit will occur when one of the three bottom lines suffers and does not meet the expectations placed upon it. Therefore a cut in costs may increase the visible bottom line, but if as an effect it reduces customer or staff satisfaction to the level where the ratio of either sinks below 1, then only Imperfect Profit has been achieved.

So our definition of Perfect P.R.O.F.I.T. is "where value is created for the shareholders, the customers and the people, in excess of their expectations, consistently over the long term". Should the triple bottom line expectations be exceeded in one year, then the next year those expectations will shift up. To keep this up over the longer term must indeed be worthy of note and a reasonable claim to 'perfection'.

Now, you will have noticed that the format of the word P.R.O.F.I.T. suggests that there are a number of parts to it. That is right. I will work through the separate stages with you. We'll make a start today."

Philip passed another of his cards to Cher, but this time there was a different message on the back.

> # To achieve Perfect P.R.O.F.I.T.
>
> **"P**repare by seeking out the key issues"

"OK," said Cher. "I see the sense of doing some diagnosis first, but I know what the key issues are. Our sales are too low and our costs are too high."

"Yes, I agree with that, but we have to go back behind those symptoms and find the causes."

They spent a long time discussing the state of the market that the business was in. By the end of it, Philip was satisfied that the market being targeted was the right one and was not under great threat. It was time for Philip to raise the main issue.

"From what you've told me, things started going really wrong as soon as you put your prices up without checking that your customers were getting enough value. What then accelerated the downward spiral was that you made it worse by putting the raw material contract out to tender and going purely for the lowest cost, no matter what the implications for quality. You've lost most of your custom as a direct result of that and nothing is going to improve until you sort out that area."

"Do you mean to say I've got to go through that tendering process again?" asked Cher.

"Probably not," said Philip. "Did you keep the tenders from the last time?"

Loyal promptly brought in the tender papers that she had filed away.

"Good, let's go through these," said Philip. "Let's forget about **Lo-Quality,** shall we? It's clear that they are not the route to success. We've got one here from **Prompt**. They guarantee delivery of your order within 4 working hours, which is quite impressive, the quality looks good and they quoted £2.50 a unit. Then you've got the original supplier, **No Hassle**, who came top on quality, had always been reasonably quick on delivery and quoted £3, but said that they would need a 12 month contract to do it at that price. What is now the most important thing to you?"

"Well, the quality I guess, although the prompt delivery is important."

"Good, let's see if they can give a guarantee on delivery times and make sure that they are still on for a 12 month contract at £3 each," said Philip.

"But that's £1 a unit more than I am paying at the moment! I can't afford it," said Cher.

"It's also £1 a unit less than you were paying before you started this," reasoned Philip.

"OK, I'll make that call," said Cher.

Just half an hour later, the deal had been done. Cher went out to give the news to the staff, or what remained of them.

"Good," said Philip. "That will make a good start. Now, while we are on the subject of cost cutting, you can get *Loyal* to re-instate all those overhead costs that went two weeks ago."

"Yes, I was going to do that anyway," said Cher. She called *Loyal* in and gave the instruction.

It was getting late in the afternoon.

"I think we've done quite enough for one day," said Philip. "Let's see what the impact of this is next week, shall we?"

"Good idea," said Cher. "I'm exhausted."

Cher was left to lock up, which was something that she had not done for many years.

WEEK NINE

Philip arrived early again the next Monday. There was no sign of Cher, so Philip took the opportunity to have another look around and talked to all of the staff before Cher arrived. In fact he did a lot more listening than talking, asking lots of questions and listening intently to the answers that they gave. He kept his black notebook open throughout and scribbled answers in a scrawl that was legible to him alone.

He was pleased to learn that Cher had been coming in each day during the week.

After having spoken to everyone he went into Cher's room and sat down, still scribbling at intervals.

When Cher arrived, *Loyal* had put the last week's figures on her desk ready. Philip, who was good at reading upside down, did not need to be told:

	This week £	Last week £
Sales (200 units at £12 each)	2,400	2,400
Materials (200 units at £3 each)	(600)	(600)
Direct staff costs (2 at £500 per week)	(1,000)	(1,000)
Gross margin	**800**	**800**
Indirect staff costs (1 at £500 per week)	(500)	(1,000)
Overheads	(1,500)	(1,000)
Cher Holder salary	(2,000)	(2,000)
NET LOSS	**(3,200)**	**(3,200)**
Philip Gabriel's 7% fee	-	-

"The loss hasn't changed," said Cher, sounding disappointed.

"Sure, there's still a long way to go," admitted Philip, "but we've taken a first step in the right direction. I think that you are ready for the next step now. I see people who are running successful businesses get this one wrong and then wonder why the business starts going backwards." He handed Cher another one of his business cards, but the message on the back was different again:

> ## To achieve Perfect P.R.O.F.I.T.
>
> **"R**ewards should be shared with all those involved"

"The next thing that I want you to do is to reduce your salary back to £1,000 per week."

"Hang on a minute," said Cher. "I see what you're up to. You've just earnt yourself £70 a week if I agree to that."

"Quite so," said Philip. "But you have been taking out an amount that the business can't afford at the moment. You're quite entitled to put it up again once I'm gone."

"OK. I'll do it but I'm not happy with it," said Cher.

"Well, that's the first part of it," said Philip. "As you're aggrieved that I would make money out of reducing your salary, the other part of this is that I want you to come up with a formula that gives a proportion of your future profits to the staff. This will be charged against profits before I take my fee."

Cher took some convincing on this point, but eventually conceded that 10% of any profits over the starting point of £1,000 per week would be paid to the staff equally. Philip suggested that they get the staff together.

When they were presented with the plan, *Supervisor* and *Disruptive* got quite excited. Then they found out that the business was losing £3,200 per week at the moment and that there was a fair amount of ground to make up before they would be due anything.

Later on, Philip and Cher got together again. "Right, the final thing for this week," said Philip, "is to get your sales effort sorted out. You can't get very far with no salesman. So let's go back to discussing *Sociable*. Are you happy to let him go to one of your competitors?"

"No, not really," said Cher. "He was the best salesman I've had here and all of the customers loved him."

"Then you'd better do what you can to get him back," said Philip.

Cher made a phone call to *Sociable*. She explained that the supplier had been changed back to **No Hassle** and that there would be a 10% bonus for the staff once the original profit level was surpassed. *Sociable*, however, was quite unwell following the experience of the past few weeks. It was agreed that he would take the week off unpaid to recuperate. In the meantime, *Loyal* would re-start the marketing programme in his absence, so that there would be some momentum going. Special letters were going to go to the customers who had recently left.

Excellent," said Philip. "You're getting back on track. I shall see you again next Monday, nice and early.

WEEK TEN

Cher arrived early on the following Monday, but was not surprised to find that Philip had been there some time before her. He was in with *Sociable* when Cher found him. *Sociable* was in quite a positive mood, having heard that in the middle of the last week, *Loyal* had received a phone call from **Hurry**, who had just received one of the mailshots. He wanted 200 units so long as they could be delivered the next day, which the staff were able to do now that they did not have to re-work the poor quality materials.

The other staff were in a better frame of mind as well. With the exception of the panic in getting the rush delivery to **Hurry**, they had not been too pushed. They had all helped with the mailshot and marketing activities, although *Disruptive* had been a bit of a problem.

A little later Cher and Philip met back in her office. *Loyal* had prepared the accounts for last week. They were as follows:

	This week	Last week
	£	£
Sales (400 units at £12 each)	4,800	2,400
Materials (400 units at £3 each)	(1,200)	(600)
Direct staff costs (2 at £500 per week)	(1,000)	(1,000)
Gross margin	**2,600**	**800**
Indirect staff costs (1 at £500 per week)	(500)	(500)
Overheads	(1,500)	(1,500)
Cher Holder salary	(1,000)	(2,000)
NET LOSS	**(400)**	**(3,200)**
Philip Gabriel's fee: (3,200 – 400) x 7% x 2 weeks	392	-

"Still a loss then," said Cher.

"Sure," said Philip. "These projects take more than a week to complete, but you can see that there has been good progress made in a short time. OK, so we got lucky with the *Hurry* order but, to be honest that was a bonus. The improvement path would have started without it. The question is, do you want me to continue for another week or shall we call it a day now?"

"No, we probably should go on," said Cher.

"Right, the first thing to do this week is to share the results of last week with the staff."

Cher began to wriggle uncomfortably in her seat. She had never shown any of the weekly results to the staff. In her view it was just not done. She had ignored all the advice to become a limited company precisely for the reason that she did not want her accounts to go on public record so that staff or competitors could not see how much she was making. *Loyal* was the only person allowed to do the accounts precisely because Cher knew that there was no way that she would tell anyone else what was in them.

"I can see that you're uncomfortable," said Philip, "but being open with your customers and staff is important if this is going to work. Let me put it this way. As far as the staff are concerned, you've told them that they will get a bonus once they exceed the £1,000 profit per week that was made previously, but do they know how close they are to it? How will your staff know that you not increasing your own salary and therefore reducing their bonus?"

"I guess so," said Cher, who didn't sound convinced. "I suppose that they do need to be motivated to do any extra work that needs to be pushed through."

"Precisely," said Philip. "If you keep them in the dark and uncertain about where they are, that alone is enough to put most initiatives off track."

So Cher went out into the workshop, called everyone together and, for the first time in all the years she had been in business, she explained the accounts to the staff. She took some questions that had obviously been bothering them for some time. Not surprisingly, *Loyal* was the only one who did not ask a question.

Later, in Cher's office, Philip got back to business.

"Right, the big job for this week is to get around to those key customers who recently left to see how they are getting on. And that is something that I'd like you to do."

"I'm sure that *Sociable* would do a better job than me," said Cher with an air of defeat. "He knows all of them better than I do."

"That may well be" said Philip, "but the message that you want to give them comes right from the top. What I want you to do is call them all and invite them out to lunch over the next week."

"But what about all the other things that I've got planned?" asked Cher. "There are some key golf society games this week."

"These meetings are more important just at the moment," said Philip. "This is the next phase of the process. The purpose of these lunches, which of course you are going to pay for, is to get them to confirm to you the reasons why you lost their business. Hopefully this will have been mainly over the quality issue, in which case you can inform them that you have taken back **No Hassle** as your single supplier and you can confirm that there were no parts returned last week as a result. Then you can see how they are getting on with their new supplier and see if there is an opportunity for you." Philip took this opportunity to pass Cher another business card.

On the back, it said:

To achieve Perfect P.R.O.F.I.T.

"**O**ffer customers the opportunity to give feedback"

"Who are you going to visit first?"

Cher got on the phone. She found that all of the ex-customers were surprised to hear from her and were so taken aback by the offer of a lunch being paid for by Cher that they agreed to meet up.

Quality was booked for the next day, *Delivery* went for Thursday and this left a gap for *Service* on Wednesday. At Philip's insistence, lunch was also set up with *Hurry* for Friday, although he was not sure that he would have time. Finally, Philip asked about *Angel*. They agreed that as *Angel* had stayed with them throughout the troubles, he should be taken out today.

"Right, I think that's enough for this week. You're going to have to move if you're going to meet *Angel*, so I'll see you next Monday at the same time."

"Is that all?" asked Cher, thinking that Philip had not done much to earn his money this week, while she seemed to be working every day.

"I think you'll find that this has given you plenty to be getting on with for one week," said Philip. "If you want something else to do, you can think about whether you have got the right staff to take you into the future."

Cher was a little puzzled by this request, but agreed to do it anyway.

WEEK ELEVEN

Philip arrived at his usual time of 7am the next Monday. This time the premises were already open. Everyone, even Cher, was at work. He went in to see Cher first.

"It looks as though you've been keeping busy. How did the lunch meetings go?" asked Philip.

"They were extremely useful," said Cher. "It was the first time that I'd met most of them. They had been just names on a sales list so far as I was concerned. To start on Monday, *Angel* was just too nice for words. I can't help thinking that he's a bit naïve really, but he said that he is always trying to keep his customers happy and never blames suppliers when things go wrong. The most interesting thing he did say, though, was that *Disruptive* does us no credit. Apparently, he's always stirring things up when he makes his deliveries. Before this all blew up, he was saying how dull it was to work in a business that wasn't moving forward. Now he's telling all their staff what a state we're in. He was even telling the

52

goods inwards staff that the parts were not up to scratch and that he expected to be back after they had the chance to work it out for themselves!

By Wednesday when **Service** had told me much the same thing, I had heard enough. I came back and set up a disciplinary hearing with *Disruptive* for the next day. I thought he'd see that the game was up and go quietly but, of course, that wasn't his style at all. He made quite a stand, but with *Supervisor* and *Loyal* coming forward with a number of instances where he had been causing trouble, I had no trouble in terminating his employment on the grounds of gross misconduct. I paid him 2 weeks money just to be on the safe side, which will cost me this week, but should help later."

"Who has been doing the deliveries since then?" asked Philip.

"Oh, I found a local courier company who will be able to help out for a bit."

"Well, how did you choose them?" asked Philip.

"Don't worry, I've learnt my lesson. **Guaranteed Couriers** were more expensive than the cheapest quote, but offered a guarantee that the delivery would be made within 2 hours, otherwise it would be free."

"Good, you're learning," said Philip. "But now you've got a van sitting there doing nothing."

"I haven't had time to deal with that, I'm afraid, " said Cher.

"No problem. We can sort it out later," said Philip. "Apart from the problem with *Disruptive*, how did the other lunches go?"

"Well, no prizes for guessing that *Quality* really put me through the mill for the poor quality issues that they have had to deal with. I got quite a lecture on the importance of quality to them and their customers. I hadn't realised that they get penalised by their customers for poor quality, so we were really costing them some money. As luck would have it, the new supplier that they went to also turned out to be getting supplies from **Lo-Quality**, and hadn't been honest enough to say this up front. They were glad to hear that I had switched back to **No Hassle** and I left lunch with an initial order of 200 units."

"Fantastic," said Philip. "Were there any problems with the order?"

"None at all. I made sure of it!" said Cher. "As for *Service*, I hadn't realised how much *Sociable* had been doing to try and keep them on-side. I took a lot of verbal punishment but, although they were impressed that I had the courage to come and see them, they said that they were happy with their new supplier and would not be changing yet."

"Never mind," said Philip. "Chances are you are the first on their list if they have a problem. What about *Delivery*?"

"Well, they also told me that *Disruptive* had been causing a problem. It seems that *Disruptive* was the barrier to us doing any further business with them, so as soon as *Disruptive* had gone I phoned **Delivery** up and told him that I had **Guaranteed Couriers** on board for the moment. They placed an order straight away!"

"Good, and what about Friday's meeting with *Hurry*?" asked Philip.

"Well, it didn't last long. He was like a whirlwind, taking mobile phone calls all the time and flying off before the end of the main course. But he did tell me what was important to him."

Just then, Loyal came in with the results from the last week. They were as follows:

	This week	Last week
	£	£
Sales (800 units at £12 each)	9,600	4,800
Materials (800 units at £3 each)	(2,400)	(1,200)
Courier costs	(1,000)	-
Direct staff costs (1 at £500 per week)	(500)	(1,000)
Gross margin	**5,700**	**2,600**
Indirect staff costs (2 at £500 per week)	(1,000)	(500)
Staff settlement	(1,000)	-
Overheads	(1,500)	(1,500)
Cher Holder salary	(1,000)	(1,000)
Staff bonus	(120)	-
NET PROFIT	**1,080**	**(400)**
Philip Gabriel's fee: (3,200 + 1,080) x 7% x 3 weeks	899	392

"Excellent! A profit!" exclaimed Philip.

"Yes, we're about back to where we started," said Cher, with a glimmer of hope in her voice.

"How have you calculated the staff bonus?" asked Philip. "With a profit of £1,080 it shouldn't have been as much as that."

"Ah, good question. I didn't think that the staff deserved to suffer for my decision to pay *Disruptive* in lieu of his notice, so I asked *Loyal* to ignore that in the calculation."

"Good move," said Philip. "You should point that out to the staff when you show them these figures. It's time to move on now. We know that you need to replace *Disruptive* to reduce the courier charges, but how is *Supervisor* getting along on his own?"

"He has been struggling," said Cher. "Each individual can only really produce 100 units per day. There have been a couple of times this week when I have come in and helped him myself."

"I thought you might have to," said Philip.

"I knew that it would only be a short term thing, so it seemed worth doing."

"It certainly is. But you can't keep doing that forever. So the question is, what is the best way of covering the vacancies?" asked Philip.

"Well, I could advertise," suggested Cher. "But that would take some time. We've got to plan what to say, book the space and wait for the paper to come out first."

"How about a faster way?" suggested Philip. "When you go out and tell the staff about the results and their first bonus payment, why not mention that you are also looking for a factory worker and a delivery driver? Say that there is a reward of one week's salary for the person who identifies someone who completes a satisfactory period of a month."

"Are you sure that's going to work?" asked Cher quizzically.

"I don't know," said Philip. "But if it works you get someone who you know will get on with at least one member of your small team."

"OK. Let's give it a try," said Cher.

The team meeting went really well. Both *Supervisor* and *Sociable* knew people who might be interested in helping out and contacted them after the meeting. Philip, his work done for the moment, went and left them to their work.

WEEK TWELVE

Philip had been away seeing relations in Birmingham over the weekend. He had arrived back at his home late on Sunday night, so when he arrived on the Monday, he was a bit later than usual. He was delighted to find that the place was buzzing. There was a lot of activity going on, with a delivery being prepared already and some new faces around. Everyone was rushing round, but this time in a purposeful way. Philip spent some time asking the staff what had been going on and soon found out that a friend of *Sociable's* called *Diligent* had been interviewed and was then offered the job of delivery driver later last Monday. In the meantime, *Supervisor* had also given Cher the name of *WorkHorse*, who had experience of doing this type of work. The thought that he could earn a bonus for his hard work was what tipped *WorkHorse* to hand in his notice at the factory where he was working and he had agreed to start with Cher today. In the meantime, Cher had been helping out as she had done the previous week.

The extra work had clearly been having a positive effect on Cher. "Come in, come in," she beamed as she saw Philip walking across the forecourt. "I've got lots to tell you."

Cher recounted how lucky they had been to get both *Diligent* and *WorkHorse* into the team. While they had been out in the market looking they had also found some other people who were interested in getting involved and had heard enough about the business to wait until an opportunity arose.

Word had also been getting out on the sales side, as the best news of all was that *Sociable* had picked up yet another new customer early last week and a further 200 units had been delivered. The extra units had been made up and sent out with the minimum of fuss.

When *Loyal* came in, the accounts looked as follows:

	This week	Last week
	£	£
Sales (1,000 units at £12 each)	12,000	9,600
Materials (1,200 units at £3 each)	(3,600)	(2,400)
Courier costs	-	(1,000)
Direct staff costs (2 at £500 per week)	(1,000)	(500)
Gross margin	**7,400**	**5,700**
Indirect staff costs (2 at £500 per week)	(1,000)	(1,000)
Staff recruitment incentives/settlement	(1,000)	(1,000)
Overheads	(1,500)	(1,500)
Cher Holder salary	(1,000)	(1,000)
Staff bonus	(190)	(120)
NET PROFIT	**2,710**	**1,080**
Philip Gabriel's fee: (3,200 + 2,710) x 7% x 4 weeks	1,655	899

"This is looking really good," said Cher. "You must be running out of things to do for us."

"Not a bit of it," said Philip. "We're only just getting started, unless you think it's gone far enough and want to get on with things yourself."

"No, I'm happy to keep going with this," said Cher. "I have to say that I was feeling this good just before things started falling apart last time, so you'd better stick around… just in case. So what have you got for us this week."

"Well, first tell me about your experience last week."

"It was a bit manic really. What with the staff interviews and the new customer, I've had to be here every day for the first time in ages. I haven't been alone either. Both *Sociable* and *Loyal* had to help out with the manufacture and packing. Remember that when we were doing 1,000 units before, we had *Greedy* helping out. I have to say that we were like headless chickens last week and I'm not sure that *WorkHorse* starting will provide all the answers."

"Just as I thought," said Philip. "But why did it take 1,200 units of materials to sell 1,000 units?"

"To be honest, that was the headless chicken syndrome," said Cher. "We wasted some materials partly because we were so disorganised and some actually got lost somewhere in the system."

"Now tell me," said Philip. "What are the plans for the rest of the day?"

"Well, we've got today's deliveries to get out quickly and then start on the manufacture for the rest of the week," Cher said cheerily.

"Is it imperative that the manufacture gets done this afternoon?" asked Philip.

"I'm not sure. Let me check with *Supervisor*," said Cher as she went out to enquire.

When Cher came back, she said "Well, he would like to try and get ahead of the game, but he agreed that it was not absolutely essential that they manufacture this afternoon. What did you have in mind?"

Philip reached in his pocket for another card:

To achieve Perfect P.R.O.F.I.T.

"Find out what ideas staff have"

Cher tucked the card into her business card wallet with the others.

"I think that with *WorkHorse* having started today, now would be a good opportunity to get everyone together and see what ideas they all have for doing the work more efficiently. I'd like to lead the session if you don't mind."

"No - be my guest," invited Cher. "I'll go and tell them. I'm sure they'll be pleased."

And so it was that in the afternoon, under Philip's guidance, the staff all highlighted the issues that had previously stopped them from being efficient.

One idea from *Diligent* stunned everyone. In only his first week, he had noticed on his deliveries that the goods inward staff at all of their customers were clearly overworked. "If only we would offer to wait while they checked the goods," he said, "we could then take the goods straight into their store room and save them a lot of trouble."

These and other ideas were added to a long list of possible solutions that were prioritised and individuals took responsibility for implementing them.

At the end of the day, Philip and Cher went through the list and made sure that the right ideas had been picked.

WEEK THIRTEEN

When Philip arrived the next Monday, things were not as he might have anticipated. Having left last week with a plan in place of what was going to happen, it was clear that very little of it had actually been actioned. The first thing he noticed was that the layout of the workshop was exactly as it had been on his previous visits. As a result of this, the staff continued to move around in all directions. There were piles of part-completed work in various places where there shouldn't have been any. Philip looked at some of the labels on the materials and it was clear that some of them were left over from last week. This was at odds with Cher's declaration that all materials that were delivered from **No Hassle** could be processed and despatched that same week.

When Philip went to try and talk to *Supervisor* about this, it was clear that he did not have the time to talk. He was in the middle of barking some orders to *WorkHorse*, who seemed to be doing a number of things, none of them effectively.

In the meantime, *Diligent* was piling goods into the back of his van, but without a great deal of care. Some of the boxes were being dropped and dented.

Philip shook his head and went looking for Cher. He found her deep in conversation with *Sociable* in his office. He knocked politely and put his head around the door. "Mind if I come in and listen," he asked.

"Yes, yes," said Cher. "Hopefully you can help us to deal with what is developing here. Why don't you fill Philip in, *Sociable*?"

"Well, the trouble started on Monday when you were taking us through that workshop. When I came out of it there was a message from a prospective customer putting in an order for 300 units. We were already behind a half a day from the workshop and, although we all knew that we had work to do to action the things that we agreed, it was just too much to turn down. We decided to leave all the improvements until the weekend after we'd made the delivery."

"Then how come it still looks as though work has not been done?" asked Philip.

"Well we worked like crazy to get the work done, but it was just too disorganised. In hindsight we should have realised that we had never got more than 1,200 units through in a week. Unfortunately, everything got stuck in the system and by Thursday it was clear that we were not going to make the extra delivery. I called them late on Thursday to tell the customer that we were going to have to let him down and I can't say that they were happy. It meant that we had to pay out compensation under our guarantee, which runs to 50% of the sale price. It's helped us to get sales in the past but we're not so happy about it now."

When *Loyal* came in, the accounts looked as follows:

	This week £	Last week £
Sales (1,000 units at £12 each)	12,000	12,000
Materials (1,500 units at £3 each)	(4,500)	(3,600)
Direct staff costs (3 at £500 per week)	(1,500)	(1,000)
Gross margin	**6,000**	**7,400**
Indirect staff costs (2 at £500 per week)	(1,000)	(1,000)
Staff recruitment incentives	-	(1,000)
Penalty for non-delivery	(1,800)	-
Overheads	(1,500)	(1,500)
Cher Holder salary	(1,000)	(1,000)
Staff bonus	-	(190)
NET PROFIT	**700**	**2,710**
Philip Gabriel's fee: (3,200 + 700) x 7% x 5 weeks	1,365	1,655

"Let's see if I understand this. We held the workshop on Monday afternoon, after which you all understood what you had to do to make the improvements that were necessary to reduce the waste and enable more units to be made. You then had a large surprise order. If you had been successful in fulfilling this order you would have produced 1,500 units in 4½ days, when the best that you have ever done is 1,200 in 5 full days. You decided to try this without making the improvements to the system that might have given you a chance of successfully making the order in the future, although there must have been doubts that you would ever be able to do this otherwise. In going ahead you risked not making the order at all and paying a 50% penalty for non-performance. From the look of things the process has been more wasteful than usual in the week, with 50% of the raw materials being lost. The overall result seems to be that you have at least one unhappy customer who did not get the delivery that they wanted. You also now have unhappy staff who have clearly worked as hard as they can only to find that their bonus has disappeared. Finally, you have an unhappy owner whose profit has fallen to less than £1,000 again. That is not to mention my own fee, which has reduced from last week. Can I remind you of one of Antonio Hemmings' unoriginal sayings at his seminar? He said that "Turnover is vanity, profit is sanity and cash is reality."

"That's a fair comment," said Cher. "I take full responsibility. It was my decision to put the improvement work on hold and go with the new order. I got carried away with the progress that we were making and thought that we could make it."

"The question is," said Philip, "if you had by some chance been successful in getting the new order out, but this week a bigger order was put in, would you be tempted to do the same thing again?"

"Possibly," murmured Cher.

"As I feared," said Philip. "If there's one thing worse than focusing on the bottom line alone, it is focusing on the top line alone. Do you remember the terms under which I took on this assignment?

The second was that if you ignore any of my advice during a week then you risk me terminating the contract immediately. After the events of this week, I must warn you that termination is now a distinct possibility. There is just one thing that I want you to remember this week." He passed Cher another business card.

On the back of it was the message:

> ## To achieve Perfect P.R.O.F.I.T.
>
> "Implementation… is what it's all about"

"The task this week is very simple," said Philip. "The plans that were agreed last week need to be implemented immediately and no new orders must be taken on until that work is complete. Have I made myself clear?"

"Yes, perfectly," said Cher sheepishly.

WEEK FOURTEEN

When Philip arrived the next Monday, the place seemed to be under better control than it had been the week before. The workshop had concentrated on reducing the amount of movement of both people and parts around the area.

The layout had therefore been altered early in the week, so that the goods inwards and despatch areas were by the doors, instead of half way to the middle, and there was a route through the workshop that the materials would follow. Philip was going to be interested to see the impact on the accounts for the week.

Cher seemed quite happy with things when he went into her office. "Things have definitely gone much smoother than normal", she noted. "It's been less hectic since we shifted everything round."

Loyal came in with the accounts:

	This week	Last week
	£	£
Sales (1,000 units at £12 each)	12,000	12,000
Materials (1,000 units at £3 each)	(3,000)	(4,500)
Direct staff costs (3 at £500 per week)	(1,500)	(1,500)
Gross margin	**7,500**	**6,000**
Indirect staff costs (2 at £500 per week)	(1,000)	(1,000)
Overheads	(1,500)	(1,800)
Cher Holder salary	(1,000)	(1,500)
Staff bonus	(350)	(1,000)
NET PROFIT	**3,650**	**700**
Philip Gabriel's fee: (3,200 + 3,650) x 7% x 6 weeks	2,877	1,365

"That's better, going in the right direction", noted Philip. "The work last week seems to have taken the waste out of the system. The question is, do you want to leave things where they are, or do you want to go on?"

"No, let's go on," said Cher. "To be honest, I'm interested to see how far you can go with this. Remember that I managed to make more than this before."

"Mmmm," said Philip. "But that was only for one week, wasn't it?"

"OK, point taken," said Cher. "What do you want to do this week?"

"Well, my question for you this week is "what extra do you think that you could get through the place now?""

"I have no idea," said Cher. "The only person who would know is *Supervisor*. Shall we ask him?"

Supervisor thought hard before he answered. "I wouldn't like to push it too hard all at once, but with more staff we might be able to double the output."

"How many staff do you need to manage that?" asked Philip.

"I think I'd need another two to make sure," said *Supervisor*.

"Two more staff! You're joking, aren't you?" scoffed Cher.

"That sounds reasonable to me," said Philip. "Remember that you had *Greedy* here when you were only producing 1,000 units. Were there any more workers that you interviewed before who looked promising?"

"Yes, there were a few," said *Supervisor*. "One of them would be needed to help me out full time in the workshop and another one would be needed to help out with the deliveries. £500 a week is a good wage around here, especially when you take into account the bonus."

"Which one would you need first?" asked Philip.

"*Diligent* has been helping out in the workshop as well as doing the deliveries, so logically it would have to be one to help out in the workshop," said *Supervisor*.

"OK, are you happy to go ahead with that recruitment?" Philip asked Cher.

"To be honest, I'm a bit nervous about it," said Cher. "If we don't get some more sales pretty soon, then you'll find the profit going down, not up."

"Don't worry. I'm coming to that now," said Philip. "We need to put the people in place first before we get the sales, otherwise the orders don't get fulfilled and customer satisfaction goes down again. I would hope that the gap isn't going to be too painful.

This brings me onto the last part of the Perfect P.R.O.F.I.T. process." Philip handed over the final card in the series:

To achieve Perfect P.R.O.F.I.T.

"Time passes, so seek fresh opportunities regularly"

"This means that periodically it pays to go back and cover ground that you think you might have covered before. Let's plan this out. Who do you think are your best customers now?"

"Well, now that we have sorted out our quality problems, **Quality** and **Demanding** are," said Cher.

"What about **Angel**?" asked Philip.

"Oh, you're right," said Cher. "He's such a good customer I always forget about him. He has to go onto the list."

"Good. Now either you or *Sociable*, or even both of you, must go and visit all of them again this week. As soon as possible really. There are two main steps to be covered.

Step one will be to make sure that everything is now all right with the quality and the service.

Step two is then to ask them if they know anyone else, not necessarily in the area, that they could recommend you to."

"Do I ask the question as simply as that?" asked Cher.

"No, that would be too crude. If you go too directly to the point then people's reaction is one of surprise and generally negative. I'll demonstrate how I do it.

Tell me, how long have you been a business owner?"

"About seven years," replied Cher.

"And I suppose that over those years you have probably met a large number of other business owners, haven't you?"

"Yes, quite a few," said Cher.

"Good. Now if I asked you to write down the names of, say, 4 or 5 of those people you could probably do that, couldn't you?"

"Yes, I think so," said Cher.

"So I could contact them?"

"I don't see why not."

Philip paused before he continued. "Please can I ask your advice? Which of those that you're thinking of should I contact first to let them know they can benefit in the same way that you have from my services?"

Cher immediately said, "Well, there's Tom Brooks of Brooks International, Michael Pickering of Schimel Enterprise and John Butterworth. They've all moaned about their low profitability to me in the past few months."

"Excellent. Now in order that it's easier for those people to take my call, it's OK to use your name, isn't it?"

"No problem at all," said Cher. She thought for a moment. "Crumbs, are they really going to go for that? Don't we have to offer them something for this? Like a discount or a cash incentive?"

"No, they tend not to work so well as professional customers can see cash incentives as a bit grubby. If they do give you a lead that works then it would be quite good to take them out to dinner or offer champagne as a way of saying 'thank you', but that tends to be enough," said Philip.

"OK, we'll do it," said Cher.

After Philip had left, Cher and *Sociable* got onto the phone and made the necessary appointments.

WEEK FIFTEEN

When Philip arrived the next Monday, he noticed that there was a new face in the workshop. *Supervisor* had brought in *Conscientious* later on last Monday. There had been a few hiccups that meant that some materials had been wasted. The workshop looked even tidier than last week, so Philip was just a little concerned that the referral plan had not worked.

When he went into Cher's office, however, her smile told the tale. She and *Sociable* had invited the three best customers out for a "thank you" lunch, and they had followed Philip's instructions. Both **Angel** and **Quality** provided a number of leads, while **Demanding** was taken off guard by the question and had to "think about it". *Sociable* chased up the leads given and recruited two of them.

The accounts looked as follows:

	This week	Last week
	£	£
Sales (1,400 units at £12 each)	16,800	12,000
Materials (1,500 units at £3 each)	(4,500)	(3,000)
Direct staff costs (3 at £500 per week)	(1,500)	(1,500)
Gross margin	**10,800**	**7,500**
Indirect staff costs (2 at £500 per week)	(1,000)	(1,000)
Staff recruitment incentive	(500)	-
Overheads and "Thank you" lunches	(1,800)	(1,500)
Cher Holder salary	(1,000)	(1,000)
Staff bonus	(550)	(350)
NET PROFIT	**5,950**	**3,650**
Philip Gabriel's fee: (3,200 + 5,950) x 7% x 7 weeks	4,484	2,877

"These look good. Are you sure you want to go on for another week?" asked Philip.

"You bet," said Cher. "To be honest, the longer this goes on, the more curious I am to see how far you can take us. That sounds a bit of an odd thing to say and I have to say that I have total confidence in you."

"I understand what you say," said Philip. "This job is getting some good momentum going and I still have a few tricks up my sleeve. Have the workshop and deliveries been under pressure this week?"

"No, not all," said Cher. "When *Conscientious* came in I took on board your last tip and we held another quick workshop. We came up with some ideas as to how to tidy the place up even more, and we implemented them, so everything ran quite smoothly. Having said that, I'm not sure how many more deliveries we could do without upsetting things again."

"Which means that the first thing that you should do is recruit that extra person," said Philip.

"Already on the case," said Cher. "The new driver starts tomorrow and a new van will be hired until I'm sure that there's enough sustainable business."

"Excellent," said Philip. "If you're one step ahead of me, then you're ahead of the game. The only other thing that I want you to do this week is take out the other customers that you did not cover last week and make sure that *Sociable* follows up all of the leads, last week as well as this week. Is that OK?"

"Understood," said Cher.

Philip had a quick tour around the workshop and talked to all the staff and was out of the door by 11 am.

WEEK SIXTEEN

When Philip arrived the next Monday, he was pleased to see that a new employee was loading a second van with parts. Philip went over and started talking to the new employee and found out that he was *Reliable*. He was a friend of *Diligent* and had been impressed by his enthusiasm about working for Holder Holdings. Having felt under-valued where he was working, he thought that he had nothing to lose by joining. Philip could see that *Reliable* was getting edgy and clearly wanted to get on with his work, so Philip moved on.

"Come in, come in," called out Cher as Philip walked past her office. "The results are here."

The accounts looked as follows:

	This week	Last week
	£	£
Sales (1,800 units at £12 each)	21,600	16,800
Materials (1,800 units at £3 each)	(5,400)	(4,500)
Direct staff costs (4 at £500 per week)	(2,000)	(1,500)
Gross margin	**14,200**	**10,800**
Indirect staff costs (2 at £500 per week)	(1,000)	(1,000)
Staff recruitment incentive	(500)	(500)
Overheads and "Thank you" lunches	(2,200)	(1,800)
Cher Holder salary	(1,000)	(1,000)
Staff bonus	(850)	(550)
NET PROFIT	**8,650**	**5,950**
Philip Gabriel's fee: (3,200 + 8,650) x 7% x 8 weeks	6,636	4,484

"Looks good," said Philip. "You've even managed to keep the waste out of the materials. I assume that the increase in overheads is due to the van hire?"

"That's right," said Cher. "Last week went really well, with some of the existing customers pre-ordering for a number of weeks in advance. That means that the hire van goes back today and the new purchased one arrives. It will cut the overheads a bit."

"Excellent," said Philip. "Now I need to be honest and tell you that my job here is nearly done and this is the point where I need to give you one week's notice of termination of our contract."

"What!" exclaimed Cher. "But I don't want you to terminate. You're our lucky charm. As long as you keep coming the profit keeps going up."

"Sure, but the principles have now been established. You've showed over the past few weeks that you have learnt pretty much what needs to be done. Don't forget, for Perfect P.R.O.F.I.T. to be achieved, all of the customers, the staff and the owners need to benefit. For me to stay on means that you are not benefiting as much as you deserve. Also, you would be depriving another business of using me on Mondays! I will come back next week for the last time and we will spend some time reviewing the principles that have been covered."

"OK," said Cher. "I'm not very happy about this, but I understand."

"Good," said Philip. "I'll be on my way." It was 10.30 am.

WEEK SEVENTEEN

When Philip arrived on his final Monday, the sun was peeping up into the blue sky and he heard the pleasing hum of machinery turning as he pulled up outside the factory in his car. As he walked in, the staff were too engrossed in their respective tasks to notice him, but as he walked through they turned and acknowledged him. He made his way to Cher's office and found her deep in conversation with *Loyal*. They carried on talking while he scanned through the spare accounts sheet that had been left for him. He was pleased to see that another customer had been recruited.

The accounts looked as follows:

	This week	Last week
	£	£
Sales (2,000 units at £12 each)	24,000	21,600
Materials (2,000 units at £3 each)	(6,000)	(5,400)
Direct staff costs (4 at £500 per week)	(2,000)	(2,000)
Gross margin	**16,000**	**14,200**
Indirect staff costs (2 at £500 per week)	(1,000)	(1,000)
Staff recruitment incentive	-	(500)
Overheads	(1,800)	(2,200)
Cher Holder salary	(1,000)	(1,000)
Staff bonus	(1,200)	(850)
NET PROFIT	**11,000**	**8,650**
Final fee: (3,200 + 11,000) x 7% x 9 weeks	8,946	6,636

"So, how have we managed to achieve this?" asked Philip. "When you tried to do this first you made the mistake of trying to organise it all by yourself. Pursuing Perfect P.R.O.F.I.T. meant that you enlisted the help of customers and staff to make the result long term and sustainable. If you look at it we've been able to do all of this by answering the questions that Antonio Hemming posed, which were:

1. How do you increase your sales volume, by getting customers to buy more or by getting more customers?

2. How do you increase the price of the units that you sell?

3. How do you reduce the costs that you incur?

Your main mistake before was that you tried to do it all yourself and keep all of the gains for yourself. You now have customers who, although they are paying more than before, are now getting a better service in return and so sales have doubled. You now have staff who are getting a bonus, which gives them 40% more than they did before and are that much happier. And as a result you have increased your profits above your starting point by a factor of 10! Everybody has won out of this.

The key learning points are that while there may be just the 3 levers to improve profitability, the way that you use them is the key to the success, not the ways themselves."

Cher handed over a cheque for £8,946. "It doesn't sound much for all the results you've helped us to achieve," she commented.

"Nonsense," said Philip. "This is quite enough. After all, it works out at less than £1,000 per day and towards the end I was doing half a day at best! What is important now is that you continue the process. The questions stay the same, but new answers are always coming along."

"I understand that," said Cher. "I've thoroughly enjoyed spending more time here and seeing the whole business improve. Thank you for all that you've done."

Just then, *Sociable* put his head round the door. "I've had a referral for another 300 units. What shall we do?"

"Let's have a think about this," said Cher.

"Excellent," said Philip. "That means that it must be time for me to go. I've got to get ready to meet Tom Brooks tomorrow. Remember? He was one of the referrals that you gave me."

Appendix: the keys to Perfect P.R.O.F.I.T.

Prepare by seeking out the key issues

Rewards should be shared with all those involved

Offer customers the opportunity to give feedback

Find out what ideas staff have

Implementation… is what it is all about

Time passes, so seek fresh opportunities regularly

And finally….

"NEVER cut costs……. if the result would be a reduction in customer satisfaction."

ABOUT THE AUTHOR

Tim Levey is a Partner and Head of Business Consulting at Reeves, a Top 30 Accountancy and Financial Services practice in London and the South East of the UK.

Reeves were the Accountancy Age Large Firm of the Year 2009.

He is the author of "Profit Improvement in a Week" which was published in 2004 by Hodder & Stoughton.

For further information of Reeves' services and to contact the author, visit **www.reeves.co**